MW00527477

Magic starts

LOVE

with you

Doggy Education for all

Peter Jam

powered by *MagicDogs.net*

LifeRich Publishing is a registered trademark of The Reader's Digest Association, Inc.

LifeRich Publishing books may be ordered through booksellers or by contacting:

LifeRich Publishing
1663 Liberty Drive
Bloomington, IN 47403
www.liferichpublishing.com
844-686-9607

ISBN: 978-1-4897-4230-8 (sc)
ISBN: 978-1-4897-4229-2 (e)

Library of Congress Control Number: 2022910640

Print information available on the last page.

LifeRich Publishing rev. date: 06/28/2022

Acknowledgments

To Hugh Taft-Morales, Niko Mamula, Elise Feibush, Jonathan Gavrin, Isabelle Gallicchio, Izabella Harutyunyan – thank you for making this dream turn into reality.

The purpose of life is to be happy But.
Happiness turns to joy when we share,
because sharing is caring,
as caring is compassion,
and compassion is a pure source of love.

Center City Spotlight

Meet Peter Jam!

By Niko Mamula and Hugh Taft-Morales

Award-winning global rights activist, composer, quadrilinguist, and professional dog behaviorist— Peter Jam does it all. On any given day, you might see him at Rittenhouse Square, training dogs or dropping by the Ethical Society for a visit. He's a fascinating person with an intriguing life story.

Jam (an abbreviation of his surname, Jambazian) was born to Lebanese-Armenian parents in Beirut during the Lebanese Civil War. His grandfather, for whom he was named, was a survivor of the Armenian Genocide, and lived in the Armenian quarter of old city Jerusalem, where Peter's father was born.

When his father was a teenager, the family moved to Lebanon. Peter was very fond of soccer as a child, so much so that he once considered pursuing a career as a pro player. He also loved animals. He didn't have any, but his uncle did.

"I always wanted to go and visit them," says Jam, "because there were dogs there." Then he discovered a new passion—guitar, realizing "it's more creative to be with the guitar than the ball."

As a teen, Jam practiced music eight hours a day and, at 19, started giving lessons. Affording lessons for himself was a struggle, however. "I come from a modest family," Jam says, "so I had to work."

His father sent him to a jewelry workshop, an "Armenian heritage thing," but Jam never lost sight of his passion for musical creativity. He formed a school band called "Vibrations"—the same name as his debut album. His love for music impelled him to look towards America, but 9/11 put that dream on hold.

After working a few years as a guitar teacher and technician, Peter Jam confronted a series of serious health challenges. In 2004 he suffered from a condition where his body was unable to regulate its temperature, causing him great suffering. He overcame that, but in 2006 he was diagnosed with stage four cancer. Hodgkin's Lymphoma was serious enough, but Peter Jam's life was put in immediate danger when his surgeon fainted during a biopsy and nearly pierced his lung. Peter survived and went into chemotherapy, which made him severely anemic – another threat to his life. As if things couldn't get any worse, in July of 2006, his city became a battle ground between Israeli war planes and the Hezbollah militants in the southern suburbs of Beirut. During the many trips to the hospital, Peter heard the war planes thunder overhead.

Surviving so many threats to his life, as questions flooded his mind, Peter had to "look deeper." From his near-death experiences, new motivation emerged. Jam began to *do* the things he had only *thought* about doing before. He adopted a new mentality, turning his concerns away from the future to live in the present. He put it this way: "You always think that you have enough time and then suddenly you wake up—oh, I'm going to die."

Peter Jam's new mission was to travel. He visited dozens of countries in Europe and around the world with his beloved dog Boogie, performing his first major peace song "If You Want." He sang and spoke out, having been given the title "Ambassador for Peace" from the United Nations Economic and Social Council (ECOSOC). Peter came to Philadelphia where, at City Hall, he was granted an honorary citation from the City Council of Philadelphia as a peace-building artist. After receiving this award, he felt a calling that Philadelphia should be his lasting home.

He was able to become a permanent resident of the United States after being awarded "Artist with Extraordinary Abilities" status. He continued to use his musical talents to promote peace at international gatherings and at the Ethical Society, where he has sung at Peace Day Philly events.

In America his passion for animals was rekindled. He worked with a German organization for animal rights, earned a professional trainer/instructor certificate in Scranton, PA, and subsequently received a pet psychology degree in the United Kingdom.

His passions exist in a cycle, "guitars, creativity, then dogs." In the midst of the pandemic, he founded *Magic Dogs,* a training and instruction service. His aim is to fundamentally change pet training from forced obedience to reciprocated trust and friendship. His relational approach to dog education intrigued Hugh Taft-Morales, Leader of the Ethical Society. With a philosophy of promoting ethics through relationship building, Taft-Morales says, "Why only focus on human beings? All sentient creatures matter."

"I don't train with treats," says Jam. "Your presence can be a reward." The crucial aspect of a relationship between pet and human is that the dog must feel it can depend on the owner or guardian. A well-behaved dog should always be looking at the owner, waiting for the owner's guidance before acting. He also pointed out an innocent yet potentially harmful mistake that some dog owners make. Because the dog is continually treated as a puppy, it is conditioned to behave as one. You wouldn't want a 60-80-pound dog jumping up on people like a puppy, would you?

Now, Jam is looking to expand *Magic Dogs* to include education for owners as well. He feels that training dogs isn't enough to truly instill a robust relationship between pet and owner. He believes that owners often indirectly reinforce bad behavior.

According to the *Magic Dogs* website, instruction provides "utmost and optimal communication." Jam notes that some people don't understand how the training works: they bring him their dog "as if it's an iPhone" with a sort of "take it and fix it" attitude. By building upon his current approach, Peter hopes to deepen the ethical connection between dogs and their owners. Say hello to him next time you see him with doggie clients in Rittenhouse Square.

Niko Mamula is an Intern at the Ethical Society, where Hugh Taft-Morales serves as Clergy Leader.

Contents

Inspiration:
The Magic Dog

LIKE MANY ADULTS, my recollection of childhood is no more than short bursts of memories and flashbacks. Throughout those memories, two things remain constant - the war and dogs.

The first dog I knew was my Uncle's, small hound mix, *Jimo*. I couldn't visit him very often due to the war, but when I did I felt a very strong bond with him. This fueled my dream to have a dog of my own.

Me & Jimo

My mother had a phobia of dogs. Growing up in the Armenian camp in Beirut, where survivors and descendants of the Armenian Genocide took refuge, she resisted having one at home and avoided them on the streets or to visit my Uncle's home. Sometimes, when I was a little kid, I used to disappear from our home only to sneak over to my uncle's to be with Jimo.

In my early teenage years I wanted to spend time with some dogs my uncle had rescued. In my early 20's, when I was a guitar teacher and technician in a music-store near the AUB (American University of Beirut) a musician friend asked me to help care for some rescued puppies. These puppies were newborns and desperately needed their mom - even though their mom was probably taken away or dead. The puppies were between life and death. I wanted to do my best to keep them alive but I had a job so I couldn't be at home in the daytime. I had to ask my mother to help make sure they were warm and well-fed for a few hours. My mom agreed and helped the puppies survive.

The puppies began to thrive, almost ready to be returned to my friend. One day on my way from work, I spotted the dog that would become my life-long companion: **Boogie**. As a labrador retriever, Boogie

Boogie

wasn't my dream dog. I was always more attracted to guarding dogs such as Doberman pinschers, Rottweilers, or German shepherds. But due to lots of reading and studying about breeds, I knew it'd be a terrible idea for my mother to live with a guard dog. It would have to be well trained which could easily take months, but a retriever or a springer would definitely be a better option for me as my first dog and for my mom to get over her phobia. It would be a win-win for all of us.

I knew I'd meet a dog like Boogie one day; he stole my heart. He was sitting in a shop but I didn't have the money to pay for him. The shopkeeper and my friend kindly let me trade the puppies for Boogie.

At first, when I brought Boogie home, my mom had trouble accepting him. I told her not to avoid him, but try to give him guidance and communicate as an indoor 'pack leader' until I came back home from work. Little by little, she learned to love him as a family member. I considered Boogie my 'son', and soon whenever people greeted me they'd ask how he was instead of asking about me.

I could never stay out late. I'd have to go home and take care of him but I was always excited to do so. I used to play with my band in pubs and clubs, and as soon as the gig was done I was delighted to go back home and take him for a walk before bed.

In the spring of 2006 I was diagnosed with cancer, but I believe Boogie knew before the formal diagnosis. He had given me different looks as if he was saying, "I know you have a big tumor inside of your body, but I am here for you." Dogs, thanks to their wolf origins - have a miraculous sense of smell that they can actually smell inside of the body. I learned this after hearing Dr. Milton Mills discuss how wolves have the ability to smell which sheep is sick or old. They can detect many diseases or even if you're pregnant.

Boogie knew that I had cancer, before the scans and biopsies. He supported me throughout the entire thing. He is one of the reasons that I am alive today.

Dogs' togetherness and social communication with humans gives us not just mental health but also improves our physical health. Recent science demonstrates that dogs help release reward and anti-stress chemicals such as 'the love hormone' **oxytocin, 'pain relieving' endogenous opioids, adrenaline, and serotonin** in both you and the pet. Our immune system will be reinforced by a hopeful and joyful state of mind. Boogie's presence with me was Magically therapeutic, saying 'I am here for you'.

When I traveled away from home for the first time, I would call and ask my parents to put me on speaker phone so that Boogie could hear me. He would recognize my voice and bark. When he heard me on a radio interview, he would start running around the house.

Boogie used to love the sea, he used to run on the beach and dive into the water. During and after my recovery we'd go relax at the beach regardless of the season. We would drive from Beirut up to Byblos (Jbeil) and relax in some place where it was deserted and calm. Boogie, my guitar, and the beach all helped me heal faster and deepen my spiritual search for purpose in life.

During those times, one of my good friends, Michael, would join us and we'd sing together, play frisbee, and try to teach Boogie how to surf. They were fun times. I was so inspired by Boogie's "magic" that I wrote a song called "*Goodboy Boogie*". It was completely unofficial, the lyrics were "peepee kaka, and tikitoto" which only Boogie understood.

In his last week alive, I was playing his song in the living room. He couldn't walk. Upon hearing the first ring of the chords he dragged himself on his belly from the bedroom to share his song with me. He wagged his tail and listened. I'll never forget those moments and how he really enjoyed his song.

After he passed away, I wanted to commemorate him by recording the song. I couldn't bring myself to play it for a while. After a few years, when the grief had subsided, I recorded the song and released it on all online music platforms, adding this verse:

> *I wrote this song to my pal*
> *His name is Boogie*
> *Such an awesome doggie*
> *He's a good-boy, brings me deep joy,*
> *Now that he's gone I call his name,*
> *Boogie'*

When Boogie passed away, my mother cried more than anyone. She credits me for helping her overcome her phobia of dogs. Give credit to "The Magic Dog," Boogie.

Boogie also taught me something that I wouldn't have been able to learn anywhere else, something so essential to the balance of my life and a deeper spirituality about humanity. He taught me to <u>love without understanding</u>. Loving without understanding is liberating. As humans, we have the tendency to strive for understanding before being able to love. Sometimes our mental faculties of reasoning or memory work against us and stand in the way of loving unconditionally. The need for understanding is our mind's way to condition every situation. Allowing only to love or be loved depends on understanding. When it depends, it's conditional. How can we love unconditionally?! How can a mother ask for understanding before loving? We try to judge the "other" before accepting and loving each person regardless of who they are. The Dalai Lama says, "Love is the absence of judgment." Boogie, and all dogs, know this and they practice it every day, every hour, and every minute. They try to teach us by practicing not by language, but by actions.

Not only do dogs have the ability to love unconditionally, but they also teach us how to do so. While touring and singing for peace in dozens of countries and cities, I was granted many awards. At one point, I was called to become a "double-country coordinator" (Lebanon and Armenia) by an inspiring global organization called *The Love Foundation*.

When I was in Orlando, the foundation asked to interview me for their program, *"Love Begins with Me."* Before we started, the interviewer asked me how I learned about 'Unconditional Love' and peace. They asked if it was living in a warzone or my experience with cancer. I smiled and told them it was Boogie. Boogie taught me these things without speaking any word or any language. Boogie could magically see things within me and helped me get in touch with myself.

Not only can dogs teach such lessons, but so can other pets or animals. In 2009 I was invited to play my peace song *"If You Want"* at a Maryland farm, and I noticed for the first time a goat being treated like an ordinary pet. I thought about how we eat animals like goats or sheep or cows. I was inspired to think about vegetarian and vegan lifestyles.

A few years later, I was having brunch in Florida with some friends and there was a lady working there that had an inspiring story which made it into local news, it was about her pig. Her pig saved her life, just like Boogie did mine but in a different way. Later on in Italy I was filming for a music video called 'All the love that I have'. There, I met a goat and horse called Jim and Lady who were living with Giulia, the video's main actress. This experience also made me think of how these animals were to Giulia like Boogie was to me. The fact is, all sentient beings are capable of experiencing pain and pleasure, having all the senses we have and above all to express unconditional love.

Inspired by Boogie, I knew I wanted to work with dogs and try to bring that magic out of them. I always believed only through inspiration can transformation happen, which is how change is inevitable but transformation optional. Let the magic shine so strongly that anybody can recognize and feel their necessity in our existence. Yes, they are "man's best friend" and family's best companion.

When I was granted the *"Artist with Extraordinary Abilities"* immigrant status and knew that I was moving to Philadelphia, I wanted to continue my education silently by approaching my next passion, which was 'Dog Training and Pet Psychology'.

I graduated and certified in 2018 as a "Professional Dog Trainer Instructor" (PDTI). I wasn't practicing much yet due to my busy schedule of touring with music and speeches. But when the pandemic hit, I had been prepared and organized for quite some time. It was only a matter of turning adversity into opportunity. I was ready to launch Magic Dogs ``Doggy Education for all" at the very start of the pandemic. The first day of lockdown I knew my new mission had begun.

Dogs are able to love unconditionally and to teach us without any words what unconditional love is. Unconditional love is essential in the world we live in. Dogs' conditional ability depends on you, your knowledge about them and their psychology '*Doggy Education*', your hard work with them 'Double Stimulation', your communication through 'Energy Foundation' and understanding 'The Zones' If you do, you will maximize your dog's abilities and bring out the magic within dogs: Dog Magic!

Introduction:
Doggy Education

SOMETHING YOU MUST understand before utilizing this booklet: most of the information offered throughout is meant for humans, to understand the doggy world.

This booklet is most effective for dog owners or guardians which I prefer to say "pawrents". Throughout the book I will use the term pawrent. You are responsible for learning to communicate with your dog in order to get the most positive results.

Most of the time, people blame their dogs for being the problematic part of the relationship. In reality, it is usually the human's behavior that causes the dog to be uncooperative or disobedient. You may not be entirely aware of how you contribute to your dog's bad behavior, so you must carefully assess your own behavior first.

Another important misconception concerns the "pack-leading" nature of dogs. Let's talk about leadership and leaders. Any leader's most basic responsibility is to provide 'Guarding and Guiding' (GG); safety and guidance bring happiness and joy. Happiness and joy are fragile. Without safety and guidance, hope, happiness and well-being can be demolished any time. If that happens, frustration, confusion, insecurity, and stress can arise. Calm, ethical, and fair leaders help us navigate through storms of life's ocean to the safety of shore.

In the dog world you cannot earn respect or trust just through words. You need to act in ways that make your 'commands' effective. Only then will dogs really feel at ease and develop a sense of safety and trust. In other words, you have to demonstrate how reliable you are, to gain your dog's respect and trust. That's what good leaders or 'pack leaders' do. To be a good leader you must be patient and calm. Your dog knows that when you're calm, you don't need protection.

Dogs are naturally "pack-leading." They descend from wolves, but over centuries they have assimilated into human families and have effectively become family members too.

So what are they? "Pack-leading" wolf descendants or human family members?! They are both. Two decades of experience with them, and keeping up to date with scientific research, shape my approach.

Dogs were originally domesticated in order to serve humans, and they still do, as search and rescue dogs, therapy dogs or security dogs. Since dogs have evolved to become our companions, a middle ground in between the two extremes is present. As a dog pawrent you must understand that your dog is both pack-leading and a member of your family. The two are not mutually exclusive.

Another way to illustrate this is through a simple two-way metaphor. As we know, all dogs are descendants of wolves. Wolves were domesticated over time and eventually became dogs. Living in the United States for a decade or so, I have connected to the "Western" or American lifestyle. However, I am still a part of the Lebanese-Armenian culture. Adaptation is a strong factor here which became quite evident when I visited Lebanon and discovered that it was somewhat difficult to re-join that community with all my love, care and respect for it.

Another example of adaptation, a Philadelphia girl whom I met some time ago in Lebanon often talked about her love for Africa. She visited Africa many times, eventually moving there, and now she loves it and wants to live there forever.

Domestication and selective breeding have made dogs human servants with a mission. Most of them have leaned more towards being family members rather than upholding the 'mission servant' position. We should avoid anthropomorphism. You need to tread carefully. Some pawrents might take it a little too far, and begin treating their dog as if it is a human child. I was actually guilty of this a long time ago with my beloved Boogie, blessed be his soul, but I now understand that we must treat animals according to their species. Your dog should be treated with all the love and care that any of your family members would get. But treating your dog like a human baby without taking into consideration dogs' senses and non-homo sapien nature, providing full time affection can turn it against you, Dogs shouldn't be getting breakfast, lunch, dinner and maybe a coffee break like a human!

Over 400 breeds (plus hundreds of mix breeds) have all been created by humans to serve. They serve humans in search and rescue, finding explosives, and even detecting COVID. Concurrently, they are our best friend, loving companion and family member.

When the pandemic hit, people began adopting dogs. It was unbelievably euphoric to read that for the first time in decades, shelters are empty. Every dog had a home. But sooner or later people started to give back their pups as things started to go back to 'normal' last summer. Shelters got filled up again. Euthensia got more common and that breaks my heart.

Treat your dog with fairness and respect. Your dog needs proper care, and proper care is less about food and short walks and more about learning and understanding the species. The last thing you would want is your dog becoming extremely territorial. Although every dog has a partly territorial nature, sometimes you can even become the territory which I call "moveable territory".

Consequently, as humans we consider this "reactive" and blame it on the dog. Meanwhile, this reality is Territoriality. The dog is programmed to either act as the protector or protected. If you don't provide protection, the dog will take on that role and protect you even if you don't want it or you don't think you are under threat. In the end, there is some kind of 'hierarchy' in place and your dog will absolutely need some sort of guidance. In human terms, dogs are equally a little kid with a 2-3 years old human mind and a territorial bodyguard that needs to be trained to stay communicated and given direction.

You must provide guidance and safety for your dog. Once you've achieved this, then your dog will start following you with full trust because feeling safe is solely connected to trust. In fact, the Turkish word for "safety" is "güven" which literally translates to 'trust' as well. This raises the question; can you trust someone that you don't feel safe with?

When dogs feel unsafe, they assume the protector role. The human needs to provide safety and guidance. Try not to be afraid - fear will lead to mistrust and mistrust will lead to conflict between you and your dog. We will discuss this more throughout the book.

Adopt a positive and friendly approach instead of rejecting the situation or interpreting as you wish. Providing guidance will directly create an interdependence in your dog's realm which the dog will gladly follow. This is the key to strengthening your relationship to achieve utmost and optimal communication with your four-legged buddy, the core purpose of 'Magic Dogs' doggy - education for all.

Double Stimulation

A DOG CAN survive on one walk and some food every day. Good care should allow your dog to <u>thrive</u>, not just survive. Some dog owners don't put enough effort into providing their dog with its necessary daily physical and mental stimulation. If this is you, don't feel exposed or guilty. I have been there too. I became aware of the importance of fuller care of my dog, and now I teach a way to implement this. It's called *"Double Stimulation."*

Double Stimulation involves both physical and mental stimulation. You can offer them indoors and outdoors; they can reinforce each other. I believe planning a routine through using 'Double Stimulation' can help you keep your beloved four-legged buddy happy and healthy. When you are caring for a dog, as the pawrent or temporary caretaker, it is critical that you plan out your dog's daily *Physical Stimulation*. In the absence of extreme weather, this can be a long walk or run, simple play, indoors or at the park or whatever fits best.

Dogs have always been active with humans. Most of the dogs are there to work, they have the physique to be active. Nowadays, since they are household companions, most of the dogs are against their true nature to be active.

If you have a 9-to-5 job, you need to take your pup and go run at least an hour in the morning for both its health and for your own. Long walks or runs, especially for puppies and high energy dogs are crucial. When it comes to choosing your pup, unless you are rescuing or adopting a mutt (which is so much full of love from your side) The purpose is to tire the dog, whatever breed or mixed breed the dog is. A tired dog is a relaxed dog, thus a happy dog.

Ralph

One day I was waiting for the elevator in a building for my next client. A guy was waiting, too. He had a beautiful large doodle **Ralph**. When he saw me he asked if I am Armenian. I am not sure how he guessed. I told him yes I am Armenian, and also a dog behaviorist. I gave him my card. He called me and we did some sessions. He witnessed the magic in a few days and we did instructing sessions as well. Everything was getting better. To focus throughout the training session, I told him to do 'Physical Stimulation' for Ralph. That was the key for all of his frustration in training. Ralph has lots of energy and without putting that energy out it is so hard for Ralph to focus, only experts can do it.

The importance of 'Physical Stimulation', which you as the pawrent can do, will create magic and is half of any training. If you have stairs at your house that can be an awesome opportunity for an indoor "play-tire circle" with a toy or ball.

I had a Facetime consultation session with a couple fostering a young pitbull from the shelter, named *Carl*. When they described Carl and how energetic the pup was, one of the suggestions I made was applying 'Physical Stimulation', in particular the stairs in their house, a great way to tire a young dog. After a few days, we had an actual session with Carl. They told me how useful that suggestion was to put that energy out with some playtime on the indoor stairs. It's inspiring how Magic starts to happen.

If your dog is socialized with other dogs and has dog neighbors that can visit each other, that's another great way for 'Physical Stimulation'.

In addition to planning this routine, you also need to balance feeding since food will only add to the dog's already existing energy.

Anything that includes action will allow your dog to put out its energy. Remember, the dog is not necessarily responsible for itself. You are responsible for your dog and doing the bare minimum will not be sufficient. As we know, dogs unfortunately do not have the mental faculties that we have in order to properly plan to take care of themselves every day.

Think of it this way: if you are sitting around watching Netflix and scarfing down pizza, you are responsible for yourself, you can get up and get some exercise. (Don't be ashamed if this rings any bells, we are all guilty of this from time to time). On the other hand, your dog is unable to do this; if the dog is overweight from 3 or 4 meals a day, and you're only taking 20-30 minute walks, nothing will change because the dog can't take care of itself! Therefore, you need to take charge and compensate.

Most dogs are active animals. They have been with humans to work all day long. Now, as most of them are just family companions, that shouldn't make them just like a teddy bear. It's okay to be lazy or out of mood some days. Your dog will feel that and be by your side. If you are not an active person, either your dog motivates you and puts you into action to have long walks and constant play moves or you might consider a cat or a rabbit that is a loving pet but doesn't require much physical stimulation as most dogs do.

Now onto the other category: *"Mental Stimulation"*. One of the best methods that you can adopt is creating little games to engage your dog. This will get their 'Clear Attention', thus earn their respect, and develop trust.

The dog's attention span can stretch from five to fifteen minutes, sometimes a little more. In my training I do five to ten minutes then a little break and then repeat it. Twenty to thirty minutes of 'Focus Time', whether it's outdoor or indoor training, is sufficient.

Remember; rewards are important, but treats are not the only reward, and might cause stress in some cases. The greatest reward is you. That's why if the dog jumps at you, you should try denying them attention. Most likely, the dog gradually will slow down such jumping and eventually stop, since it's not getting your attention.

Since your attention is important, how you get the dog's 'Clear Attention' is essential and basic to earn 'respect' which simply is 'I see you, I value you'. The timing matters.

It starts with the name. You have to call the dog's name five times and see how many times they look at you this is to check or test how much the dog will give you 'Clear Attention' which sooner or later will turn into earning 'respect'

To check the development of respect, try 'come' five times when your dog is distracted or in the other room and record after how many times the dog will hear your voice, listen and come. Which is 'Clear Attention'. The sooner she does, the greater respect and trust you've earned.

You can also test this by creating a distinct type of whistle or other sound. A high frequency sound is best, which is why whistling works well. Even if you can not whistle, just a sound that the dog's ear can catch. I have created more than one unique whistle that serves as a kind of language between me and my dogs or any dog I work with. Your voice commands can be in your normal tone of voice.

Then you can say 'come' and/or whistle and see if they will come. If they don't, you can try putting a long leash on your dog and hiding a treat in your hand. You should use the leash as a <u>guiding tool</u> - don't pull the dog towards you. You can give a gentle brief tug to encourage them to come. When they do come to you, reward them with a simple 'Goodboy/Goodgirl' or a little treat. Remember, the goal is to program your dog to look at you, not at the treat. You are training them to give you respect.

I can tell you a little story about a cute cockapoo named **Cosmo**. Cosmo's pawrents had another doodle dog, **Luna**, when Cosmo came to the house. In this case the dog can copy the other dog as well, but when I met Cosmo he didn't like to be touched or carried. He growled when I tried to hold him. Growling is a warning sign telling me 'I have been hurt before, how can I trust you, you won't hurt me?' To listen to this voice you have to put extra importance, effort and care. First, to gain some trust. Then, to go forward and do the things you want to do. So I applied 'Mental Stimulation' in short sessions which is a mix of 'Focus time' for 5 minutes then 'Play time' for 10 minutes. Little by little Cosmo started to trust me. I became his best buddy. He allowed me to hold him even, to cut his facial hair, the hair blocking his eyes. This reflected on how he felt safe with me around other dogs.

One day I got a call from a new client. I wanted to go meet them but Cosmo was with me. I asked Cosmo "Be a Goodboy" even around the new pup that is having behavioral issues. Guess what? After meeting them, the pawrent told me "I want our pup to be like Cosmo'. I said 'Yes'. That's what happened. Cosmo's parents were so happy and proud of his inspiring transformation.

One lesson I teach is about practicing patience. I call this the "*Patience Exercise*".

Try this yourself. Put your dog on the couch and tell the dog 'stay' as you back away about six feet. If the dog doesn't stay on the coach, use a leash to guide them back. Repeat this until they follow your voice commands and then reward them with a treat or just by voice. Repeat the process. Start with five seconds and gradually increase the time between the initial command and the reward. Then, apply the same gradual increase with distance. This exercise will calm the dog and help them overcome separation anxiety. It will also develop greater trust and will help the dog be less anxious.

Often, indoor training can be best for "Mental Stimulation" exercises. There are less distractions for both dogs and humans so they can both be more focused and less anxious. When humans have more relaxed energy the dogs can reflect that. Outdoor training can be more challenging.

When it comes to collars and tools, you should avoid electric shock or choke (aka prong) collars and halters. Sometimes these collars are used to solve extreme problems, but they should be used for only a short time period. These are "confining tools" which use negative reinforcement. "Confining" your dog won't solve most problems and will keep you and your pup in the "Struggle Zone" forever (see chapter 5 'The Zones'). While they might help "train" the dog about a certain practice, there's a big price to pay regarding the dog's health and well-being. These devices don't enhance your dog's happiness and well being and are not recommended to be used on a daily basis and you will notice your dog's annoyance.

I recommend a regular collar and a leash, not harnesses which are pulling tools for sled dogs. You can use them, but only after creating good communication.

Crates can serve their purpose for dogs between the ages of 3 to 8 months. At 8 months, the dog has full awareness and capacity to understand what it is to be gated or crated and connect it to being suppressed. Their crate should be doorless as if it is a little haven for them so that they can go in and out with no stress and without being suppressed. Meanwhile the indoor boundaries should be invisible. Which can be practiced by a long leash, until the dog is fully accustomed to your voice and energy.

An example that illustrates the problem with using crates to affect behavior, there was a couple living near the City Hall with a 4-month old golden retriever that looked like a teddy bear. They called me urgently requesting my help when their puppy turned into a big teddy bear that lunged at people on the street. This was due, in part, because they allowed people to greet their dog on the street, which programmed the dog to do the same with great energy. When I started the training, I realized that the dog was being confined in his crate, with only a few breaks and a short walk. The pawrents were afraid the dog would destroy things in the house. Being so confined, the dog developed a phobia about the crate. I removed the door from the crate to help the dog get less afraid of it. It helped the dog relax and gain more trust, which improved his behavior outdoors.

For high energy dogs there isn't any cure or solution other than 'Physical Stimulation". Be wary of any drugs or pills which are marketed as "calming" tools. Most of them probably have negative side effects. Most dogs are put on these sedative medications due to their high energy or hyper behavior. It's better to use 'physical stimulation' and 'mental stimulation' to transform your pups 'negative energy' so they can be calm and happy naturally. Taking away your dog's energy with a pill might be a short cut, but the consequences could be catastrophic.

I encourage pawrents to help align the mind and body of their pups. In Lebanese we say "Akl el Salim bi Jesm el Salim," which means, "healthy mind in a healthy body". You can nurture healthier minds and bodies when you focus on their interaction with "Double Stimulation" practice. It may take some time, but achieving an adequate balance between the two will most definitely result in positive progress.

The beauty of this training is its casual and simple nature. You are effectively allowing your dog to be dependent on you, while also earning mutual respect. Although it might sound demeaning or harsh, you want this type of dependence. You don't want your dog to completely take the lead. It can remain your companion and friend, but still look to you as the leader or guide.

Energy Foundation

ENERGY, SOME MIGHT call it body language but it is more than 'body'. I believe it's vibrations, the soul, the aura, the spirit of any sentient being.

Sometimes your intuition senses when someone is 'down' without any words. Sometimes, even over the phone, just hearing someone's voice you would know how they really are.

Energy, like dogs, doesn't lie. Dogs are always in the present moment. Their energy is so apparent it is the reflection of the moment. Dogs don't have human mental abilities like imagination, perception, reason, and so on. This is the dividing factor between humans and non-humans. Ironically, these intellectual advantages we are so happy to have, often lead us to anxiety and stress. We are so concerned about the past and worried about the future that we abandon the "here and now". Meanwhile, happiness and sorrow are experienced in the 'here and now'. Dogs don't need to meditate or do yoga in order to deal with their negative emotions. So, the immediate energy of dogs dominates their behavior.

Like human beings, dogs have moods, either high or low energy. Both have healthy and unhealthy traits. When a dog has low energy, it feels calm and safe. Remember, sometimes if a dog is sick it reflects 'low' energy.

When a dog has high energy, though this can be cheerfulness, it often indicates that they feel anxious or overexcited. In most cases, you can observe a dog's energy beyond its body language. Sometimes over-simplified analysis of body language does not accurately determine the dog's energy. When a dog's tail is wagging, almost everybody would say that this implies happiness. But you need to assess the dog's overall energy and avoid over-emphasizing just one element.

TJ

I spent a few weeks past summer training **TJ**, a mixed-breed rescue that came from Tijuana. TJ's tail was always wagging, which turned out to be quite deceiving. He was anxious, unfocused, and therefore unsafe or insecure. He also had high energy. In this situation, the course of action I took was calming down his high energy and reinstating strong focus through '*Communication and Encouragement*' and magic happened.

Reina, a two year old labrador, had a similar issue. She was very overexcited, and that led to her being stressed or unfocused. I started to build my relationship with Reina by earning 'Clear attention'. Even without a treat, which is 'respect', I upgraded our communication to let her feel safe,

Reina

developing trust and feeling relaxed especially outdoors. We practiced 'Mental Stimulation 'and also, I kept watching my energy to be mostly calm and relaxed so that she could calm down and focus better– Magic happens!

There is a thin line between anxiety and overexcitement, though both are high energy. High energy severs the communication between dog and pawrent. The dog is so unfocused that it essentially cannot hear you. There are several ways to determine whether or not your dog has high energy.

In traditional obedience training, dogs tend to follow commands but they might remain high energy regardless. Here, there is a risk of losing 'control' over the dog due to high energy. You need to establish 'respect' or 'Clear Attention' so that the dog is not obeying you under stress. You can easily test if they are stressed by the way they take a treat. The dog will aggressively *grab* the treat if there is high energy because the dog is under stress. I have called this exercise "*Kindly and Gently*". The challenge is to be so relaxed that the dog reflects that energy and would take the treat "Kindly and Gently".

To train your dog effectively, you must be calm. Take longer, slow breaths yourself. You can see its soothing effect on your dog. Just try to breathe heavily next to a dog and see how the dog gets troubled. Then try relaxing and breathing slowly and the dog will mirror that energy.

What you want to avoid is a 'gold digging' cycle where we condition the dog <u>exclusively</u> with food or treats. Focusing on energy, instead, can be a crucial way to build a deeper level of communication with your pup. It might be hard at first but by applying the '3 Ps' (*Practice, Patience, Persistence*), we can witness the Magic.

But there is a catch! You can only provide calm energy once *you* are calm. Dogs mirror your energy and project it back to you. Personally, I am challenged by this in my training. There are times I have high energy. I need to forget about the dog, take a step back, and look at myself! Communication starts with the pawrent, especially in stressful situations.

Say you are walking your dog, and you anticipate that your dog might bark at another dog coming towards you. Often, you are the first one to tense up, and so the dog copies you. If you are nervous and start giving commands like 'Sit', you effectively confirm that there is a threat, even though there isn't one.

Imagine a soccer team: eleven players, one captain on the field. If the captain seems nervous, then all the players will reflect that and be nervous themselves. If the captain is confident and provides guidance to the team, the opposite occurs. Tranquility leads to trust, and with trust comes safety. This is the cycle you want to reinforce. The goal, always, is to allow your dog to trust you and be safe with you. It is the pawrent's awareness and responsibility to develop a trusting atmosphere for their dog.

I needed the three P's in my work with a beautiful Yorkie mix pup **Fritzy**. Fritzy had ball possession and other traits that might cause problems indoors,

Fritz

especially with a young child in the house. I began with outdoor sessions and they improved indoor communication. Fritzy was a rescue and never allowed humans to touch his paw. He even learned to give me the 'Paw' which the pawrent had considered impossible. It was inspiring to witness the Magic of transformation through the development of communication with calm, chill and cheerful energy.

You must be conscientious in your training. You are the captain and the dog should be relaxed and happy to follow your lead. Abide by: *'Practice, Patience, Persistence'*. Don't forget them. They will get you to your goal.

The Zones

IN MANY ENCOUNTERS with dogs, there are two zones: the '*Struggle Zone*' and the '*Safe Zone*'.

The 'Struggle Zone' is where the dog encroaches on you or you get into some kind of challenge, like tugging on the leash. There are people that have had a dog for several years and are still trapped in the 'Struggle Zone'.

Breaking the 'Struggle Zone' and reprogramming your dog come with 'Mental Stimulation'. By practicing 'Mental stimulation' you can build trust and create a trustworthy interdependence. That allows you and your dog to enter the 'Safe Zone'.

Both the 'Struggle Zone' and the 'Safe Zone' exist in relationships between dogs as well. In dog to dog socialization there are also three separate phases: *Conflict, Avoidance, and Friendship.*

Conflict occurs when two dogs meet and they do not get along. Currently I am fostering and training **Lanu**, a rescue Jack Russel terrier mix from STAR (Street Tails Animal Rescue). Lanu has had problems with

Lanu

being 'reactive' but has made decent progress over the course of my training. I'm also training a one-year old, **Tater-Tot**, a golden doodle who is still learning and progressing every day.

Tater Tot & Twyla

When these two first met, there was a conflict which I immediately broke up. They started to avoid each other, so I took them on a walk together to ease the tension between them and establish myself as a leader. I took them to Rittenhouse Square, actively making sure they felt safe with me. They slowly began to socialize and greet each other, eventually becoming best friends.

Twyla, a sweet and sociable springer spaniel therapy dog, is also best friends with Tater-Tot. Twyla helped Tater-Tot to properly socialize, and Tater-Tot carried that over to Lanu. This series of changes represents the importance of dog socialization.

In situations where you think there may be a clash, you have to be prepared but not anxious. Your anxiety will affect the dog and possibly make the conflict worse. Being calm and confident as an pawrent will help them improve their attitude towards other dogs.

Chase   Attlee

Two other dogs I've worked with, **Chase** (a border collie) and **Attlee** (a whippet), have similar dynamics. Ironically, Chase is hyperactive, high energy, and Atlee is super relaxed, low energy, but neither is interested in playing with other dogs, they immediately go to the avoidance phase. As explained in the previous chapter (Energy Foundation), they are not afraid of the other dog, but clearly have no interest in playing. They are more focused on the main leader to give guidance or a ball/toy.

Avoiding isn't necessarily bad. As long as there are no clashes, avoiding is a step in the right direction towards socialization. Socialization is one of the main things I work on in the city, where many pawrents are unaware of how to manage 'the Zones.' When the dogs are socializing, often people have more fear than the dogs. If pawrents can understand 'the Zones' and watch their energy, they can help their pup socialize better.

Usually, when a puppy is 2-3 months old, pawrents bring them to their dog park to socialize, which I do not recommend. Simply because the success is 50/50. It's better to find a 'passive' dog for that puppy or another puppy because we don't want bad experiences to overpower the puppy, causing fear and anxiety anytime seeing another dog.

Something that happens in dog parks is 'humping,' which often makes people feel very uncomfortable. They may feel that these sexual displays will become a form of animal rape or lead to a fight. They immediately jump in to distance the dogs from each other. My advice is to give it a few seconds and see.'Humping' can be many things, including boredom or play. We need to learn how to read the energy of the situations, and not get caught up in rigid thoughts. It's fine to be cautious but it's not always something that needs immediate human intervention.

BD & Cosmo

'**BD**,' aka "***Best Dog***", a rescue boston terrier that's quite 'passive' when it comes to socializing, has an inspiring story. The pawrent told me they thought that 'BD' might have had bad experiences with other dogs. Even though the humans BD interacts with are friendly, around other dogs BD gets nervous and often runs away.

After we started training BD with deep 'Communication and Encouragement', she showed us lots of Magic. She didn't just go to the dog park to play with other dogs. She seemed driven to get to dogs that were timid and afraid. She got close to those dogs and helped them move from the 'avoidance' phase to 'friendship' phase. In helping those dogs get into the 'safety zone,' BD became my 'Partner in Crime,' or, perhaps better, my 'Partner in Mission'.

Always be aware that the 'Safety Zone' starts with you, within yourself. If you are not feeling safe your pup won't feel safe. What is important about 'Doggy Education' is that it is more for the pawrent than for the dog. It instructs you how to balance your energy, correct your 'Positioning,' and communicate with your pup.

'*Positioning*' is basic for dogs. Yet most of the time we don't pay attention to how we can create the magic just by fixing our position. This often happens while walking your dog. In the city I teach what I call the 'U' leash walk, also known as 'Loose leash' walk, when neither your dog nor you is pulling and there is no tension on the leash. The more tension, the weaker and less effective is our guidance. It can lock you up in the 'Struggle zone.' Breaking the tension is what you need. Positioning the dog in an invisible circle next to you, constantly practicing communication, and correcting through unpredictable walks and sudden stops with a hidden treat in your hand and a quick tug on the leash as a quick reminder as if you are poking your friend's shoulder. Immediately, reward with voice or treat. Practicing 'U' leash technique with just a regular collar will eventually get you to lose the tension and make your pup relax, following your verbal and behavioral guidance, thus moving you from the 'Struggle Zone' to the 'Safe Zone' of mutual communication and understanding.

Holding or carrying the dog on your lap or standing next to the dog makes a big difference in how 'reactive' the dog behaves. Too often we blame the dog. With a little bit of 'Doggy Education' in 'Positioning' you will see your pup is innocent. Correcting your position is crucial many times. Just correcting my position made the dog feel safe and everything set into place.

Icarus

Last spring, a professor contacted me for training services for a beautiful springer spaniel named **Icarus.** He told me that Icarus was 'reactive' when seeing other dogs or people passing by while standing outdoors watching people and dogs pass by. The Pawrent unknowingly positioned Icarus between his feet. I wanted to see how the dog would 'react.' As soon as I noticed the dog between his feet, I instructed him to put Icarus on the side of him. Sometimes pawrents don't realize 'positioning' can make their dog more territorial, thus making them what I call a 'moveable territory'. This is 'indirectly reinforced behavior' from the pawrent, a common cause of doggy behavioral problems that exist.

I also work with dogs and Pawrents to teach them about 'Desensitization and Normalization'. The first, being the 'Struggle Zone' and the second, the 'Safe Zone'.

When working with dogs, you should be aware that they may have pre-existing fears, such as fear of thunderstorms or fireworks. You need to create safety in a chaotic environment which can only come from their trust in you. You cannot simply remove these fears, but you can teach the dog that they can overcome through courage that comes from their trust in you which I call 'Communication and Encouragement'. Introducing the trigger or fear should only be done once you have assured the dog that trusting you is true safety.

For instance, if there is a trigger, don't hug an anxious dog. By doing this, you are sending the message that the trigger is real. Instead, practice 'Mental Stimulation' redirecting the energy to increase the focus so the dog feels safe. Using this method, you can empower your dog to trust you while in a chaotic environment.

Here's an example of 'desensitization.' Two dogs, **Ruey** and **Darwin**, a French bulldog and a Shiba Inu mix, were anxious about the doorbell,

Ruey & Darwin

the TV animal sounds, and the sound of barking dogs. They would react to these sounds by barking nonstop. So, I practiced "Mental Stimulation" to earn their 'Clear Attention' and make them feel safe. After that, whenever they heard those triggers they stopped frantically barking, relaxed, and looked at me for guidance. There was no more being 'reactive' as pawrents often describe.

Sometimes I practice outdoor 'desensitization,' which I did recently with Tater Tot. If puppies develop fear and anxiety around trucks, don't run away from the threat or hug the dog. That signals that there is a reason to be afraid. Instead, face them calmly and practice 'Mental Stimulation' giving direction, thus providing protection. This teaches them that it is okay for the truck to be there and that it is not threatening our safety.

Over time, I developed trust with Tater Tot. When the garbage truck was around, we approached it to desensitize him. I showed him that it's okay to be non-reactive to the trucks, by taking the focus and making him feel safe. I rewarded him and encouraged him as we got closer. Soon the one million dollar moment happened, when he was not scared anymore. We normalized the situation and are in the 'Safe Zone.' That's the Magic.

It's all about understanding 'The Zones' and helping your dog move from the 'Struggle Zone' into the 'Safety Zone'. This will calm both your dog, and yourself!

The Approach

IN 2009, I was a music teacher working with a teenage girl rock band. One day while driving to the studio with the band, I had to stop at the local pet shop to pick up some stuff. At that moment some of the teens went to the next room in the petshop and called me to see a cute Jack Russell terrier in a crate. What I saw I could not unsee. **Spotty** was in a very bad situation, dropped in the cage with other pups. His skin was scratched raw and one ear was bitten. He looked hopeless, sad, and anxious. The minute he saw me he said, 'I know you can take me away from here'. I heard and I could not unhear his silent words. After a sleepless night, I went back the next day. Since I couldn't adopt him, I proposed a deal to help Spotty. My deal was to take Spotty to the vet, treat him and bring back. The pet shop owner refused. He wanted me to pay to take Spotty and then return him to get my money back. I couldn't say no, I got Spotty and he stole our hearts. We never went back.

Boogie & Spotty

My mother also loved Spotty. When I was away touring in the states, she would tell me Spotty was always ready for food at 5:59 PM every day. That was his 'Foodies Time' and he knew it. Spotty surprised my mom by how communicative he was. Other dogs have different ways of signaling their needs. **Cash**, a dog I worked with in Society Hill, would scratch the back door when he wanted to go out. As you open the door he would go do his thing and

Dixie & Cash

come right back in. So he knew what he wanted, to go out and immediately come back.

It is always healthy to stick to a routine and that routine has to be created by you. A dog can understand the approximate time to eat, when to go out and when, where and what's next on the daily routine. I recommend that you help the dog understand a schedule by dividing time for your dog so as to create their routine. For example, I designate these categories: 'Foodies Time,' 'Poopies Time,' 'Play Time,' and more.

Regarding 'Foodies Time,' feeding your dog is an activity itself. Don't leave food out all the time thinking that it is a good thing to allow the dog to eat whenever they please. The smell of food changes if it's out for an hour or two and dogs, who have heightened sense of smell might lose interest in the food you offer.

Stella

'Poopies Time' or 'Peepee Time' is when the dog has a potty break. **Stella** is a beautiful bird dog in Queen Village that I have trained to 'pee on command.' Also, I trained my lab Boogie to bark on command (he even won a prize in the local dog show in the "Most Vocal" category). Now, if I say 'Hache' which means bark in Armenian, he barks once. When I say 'Hache' twice, he barks twice. The European Kennel Club representors were amazed. While this might seem crazy, it's simply the result of good communication, encouragement, and practice with a routine. Once it's done successfully, reward and repeat.

As you create a routine for your dog around these 'times', I encourage you to talk with your dog as you would talk with your brother, sister, or any human friend. At first the dog might not know your language, but eventually will understand some of what you're trying to communicate. You may be surprised by how much dogs can understand from your words and the tone of your voice.

Years ago, I had an old convertible VW beetle which Boogie loved. When I went into a store for 10-15 minutes, Boogie waited for me patiently. I saw someone approaching him and I ran out. The person said to me, 'I learned that Dobermans save 53 words, how many words can your dog save?' I smiled and said ``He knows four languages, yes he does understand all the languages I speak." Though he was surprised, it was true. Scientific articles explaining this are coming out regularly.

People are often unaware of the reality of doggy behavioral issues; people often look at their dog as if it were a broken car. They just take it to a training camp and essentially say: "fix it". When the dog comes back, it might seem as if it was "fixed". But as time passes, the dog goes back to its habitual cycles in the same environment, unless training continues from the pawrent and whoever lives with the dog.

Dogs should be treated differently so that they feel safe, even more than feeling affection and love. Love and affection without developing trust can turn possessive and create problems.

A friend's sister who got a puppy was unaware of this. The puppy didn't know indoor boundaries and had very high energy. My friend told me that they sent him to a ten day training camp to 'fix' this problem. When he came back, it seemed the problems had been 'fixed' but soon he was more aggressive than before because he felt unsafe. The sister didn't really know what the trainer was doing.

She couldn't keep going with the anxious puppy, so they called me. I told them the problem was not with the puppy. I recommended a calm but assertive approach until they regained the dog's trust. As the dog starts feeling safe Magic happens.

Training is the daily communication of you with your dog. Nobody else can do it for you. A trainer might instruct you but eventually you have to do your part in it and that's how the real Magic happens between you and your pup. Training is only half of the process; the other half is instructing the pawrent to continue the training correctly.

It is crucial for the trainer to instruct the pawrent about 'Physical Stimulation' as well as 'Mental Stimulation', the basis of any effective training.

Over the summer, I got a booking from a couple living in Dallas, Texas with three dogs. I flew out, stayed with the dogs for a few days, and I "fixed" all the bad behaviors they were exhibiting. I knew that when the pawrents eventually came back, they might revert the situation to its initial state. So, I stayed for a few extra days to instruct them how to practice on their own. I demonstrated how I work on my energy while communicating with the pups, correcting myself before correcting the dogs' behavior. It was a truly fantastic experience.

A few weeks after I came back to Philadelphia, I got a call from them. They said the dogs were amazing. This is why the pawrents need to play the key role in the training process. It doesn't just end once the trainer is finished. I would say it starts there. The experience in Texas is what I would call the "rehabilitation process" in which I go to the dog's living environment. I rehabilitate to form an entirely new way of living, from eating, to going out, creating a healthy routine, a complete communication and schedule for the dog. This happens without the pawrents. After days or a week, they can come and join. Gradually, I pull myself off the scene and let the pawrent do what I am doing by instructing them.

My typical training session is 20 to 30 minutes, or sometimes more, depending on the session on a daily basis merging in instructing the pawrent. If there is more than one person, I prefer to work with one person at a time because it makes everything faster and easier. This process sees progress in only a few sessions, the real transformation coming when we tap into the dog's habitual cycle which is 21 days. As I substitute myself for the pawrents to become the customized trainer of the pup. Then I might see the dog once a week for a short session or a socialization session with other dogs.

Dogs and especially puppies often pull you to whatever they are smelling, maybe even a mile away, and they can grab, chew and swallow toxic stuff on the ground. It can be from a piece of pizza or chicken dropped a few weeks ago. It can put your innocent pup in the hospital and cost you a lot.

From my days battling cancer I learned prevention is the key and worth ten times the treatment. Prevention is best, for example, when you see another dog coming and the dog is jumping on people or lunging, barking, you can communicate with your pup to stay in focus practicing 'Mental Stimulation'. You need to prepare for this at home (indoor training), as if you were going to gym and exercising to be stronger. You can work with your pup just 5 minutes a day and keep the problem away!

Through practicing 'Double Stimulation', watching your energy, ('Energy Foundation) and exercising the three P's, 'Practice, Patience, Persistence,' you can transform a dog in as little as 3 weeks. (21 days of habitual cycle) You have to create a robust routine that you and the dog can follow in tandem. The dog needs to be aware of what time it is, part of the routine. On the other hand you should know when you are in the 'Struggle Zone' to work towards the target of the 'Safe Zone'.

You can utilize this book as a guide for yourself in your day to day life. Work on bringing your mind and your body into the moment. Dogs live in the moment, in the here and now. Once you learn to do that for yourself, you will align your mind, and your body. All the stress and anxiety start to fly away. You will be relaxed and your dog will be happy when you are relaxed. Magic Dogs are happy pups!

This book can be helpful whether you have a dog or not. Magic happens the minute you believe in magic, and magic starts with you.

My hope and wish for you is to use this booklet as a guide to begin a movement that starts with you and me for our beloved best friend and family companion. The dream is to see every pawrent take the time to work on her/himself and experience the true magic of dogs. I am lucky to get inspired by them every single day. In the end, it is all about inspiration that we can bring true transformation. Inspire to get inspired. It's a circle. This cycle of Magic happens with you and me, my friend. This magic leaves us speechless every day, the Magic Dogs.

CPSIA information can be obtained
at www.ICGtesting.com
Printed in the USA
BVHW030212180722
642393BV00011B/287